This is

_____

story

Encountered an Issue? Let Us Know!

We take great pride in creating our journals with care and attention to detail. However, if you encounter any issues such as printing errors, faulty binding, or other defects, we are here to help.

Please don't hesitate to contact us at support@mightymammothpress.org, and we will ensure you receive a replacement copy promptly.

Copyright Notice

Father, Share Your Story
ISBN: 978-1-913485-46-7
© 2024, Mighty Mammoth Press. All rights reserved.

No part of this book may be reproduced, distributed, or transmitted in any form or by any means, including photocopying, recording, or other electronic or mechanical methods, without the prior written permission of the publisher, except in the case of brief quotations embodied in critical reviews and certain other non-commercial uses permitted by copyright law.

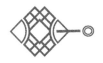 # CONTENTS

My Time Capsule	5
Early Years	10
Childhood	16
Becoming Yourself	21
Teen Life	27
Beginning Adult Life	40
Adult Relationships	49
Adulthood	56
The People Who Shape Us	67
Fatherhood	74
Reflections	82
Notes to Loved Ones	86
Fun Insights	90
Notes To Family	98
Notes To Friends	110

Fatherhood

Being a father is a lifelong bond that remains unshaken by time or distance. No matter how old your children are or where life takes them, the connection endures. Fatherhood brings purpose, stability, and meaning.

A Constant Presence

Fathers may not always hear it, but they are always in their children's hearts and thoughts. As children grow, they lean on their father's support, approval, and love.

The Quiet Strength of Fatherhood

And it goes both ways! Fathers spend their days wondering and caring about their children's well-being and happiness. Though often unspoken, a father's role is invaluable, shaping the family's foundation with quiet strength—just as vital as the air we breathe.

My Time Capsule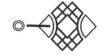

"A father's love builds bridges no one else can see."

Birthday

What is your birthdate?
....

What was your full name at birth?
....

Do you have a second name?
....

What was your length and weight at birth?
....

Were you born in a hospital? If not, where?
....
....

In what city were you born? Do you still live there?
....
....

How old were your parents when you were born?
....

My Time Capsule

"Strong, steady, and steadfast — that's a father's heart."

Family Tree

Were you named after a relative or someone else of significance?

....

Did any family members visit when you were born, such as uncles, aunts and grandparents?

....

Did you have a large family with many cousins and uncles and aunts?

....

Did you already have a sibling when you were born or were you the first child?

....

How did your parents describe you as a baby?

....

....

....

....

My Time Capsule

"Fathers give us roots and teach us to reach for the sky."

First Year

What events were going on around the world on the day you were born?

....

....

What makes the year or day you were born special or significant to you?

....

....

Do you know what the first toy you were given was? Who gave it to you, and do you still have it somewhere?

....

....

What were some popular movies that came out the year you were born?

....

....

....

My Time Capsule

"The wisdom of a father is the light that guides his children."

What was a hit song that was in the charts that year?

....

....

When did you first sleep through the night? Have you been told if you were a good sleeper as a baby?

....

....

What was your first favourite food? Was there anything you refused to eat?

....

....

....

....

Did you go to any baby groups or do any activities with other babies?

....

....

....

 # Early Years

"A dad is a child's first hero and the world's quiet rock."

First Memories

What is your earliest memory?

....
....
....
....
....
....
....
....
....
....
....
....
....

 # Early Years

"In a father's arms, we feel safe, loved, and ready to conquer."

Is there a photograph that really reminds you of being a small child?

....

Do you know what your first words were? Was there a reason these were your first words?

....

....

....

At what age did you first go on holiday? Who did you go with and what did you do?

....

....

....

Do you remember one of your favourite places to go to as a young child?

....

....

....

 # Early Years

"Fathers are the compass that points us to a better future."

What special events or holiday activities do you remember?

....
....
....
....

Can you remember what your favourite meal was as a child? What foods did you not enjoy?

....
....
....
....

What were your favourite things to do? What games did you enjoy?

....
....
....
....

Early Years

"Every dad carries a piece of his children in his heart."

How old were you when you started to walk?

....

When did you lose your first tooth? How did you celebrate it?

....

....

....

....

....

Do you know what your first words were?

....

....

....

....

....

....

Early Years

"A father's strength lies in his gentleness."

Family Life

Did your family have any special traditions to celebrate your birthdays?

....

....

Did you share a bedroom with anyone, such as a sibling?

....

....

If you were an only child, did you enjoy it? If not, did you get on well with your siblings?

....

....

Did you live in the city or the countryside?

....

....

Were you the only young child in your family?

....

 # Early Years

"Dads hold our hands for a while but stay in our hearts forever."

What kind of personality or nature did you have?

....

....

....

....

....

Did you have a lot of cousins and family members around you when you were young?

....

....

Where did you grow up? Was it the same place as where you were born?

....

....

....

....

....

Early Years

"A father's love never asks; it only gives."

Are there any funny stories you have been told about your first years?

....

....

....

....

....

....

....

....

....

....

....

....

....

....

 # Childhood

"Dad – the man who can fix anything with just a look."

Childhood Friendships

Can you remember the name of your first best friend as a child and how you became friends?

....

....

....

....

What was special about your childhood friendships?

....

....

....

Do you think that childhood friendships last longer than adult friendships? Why?

....

....

....

....

Father, Share Your Story

 # Childhood

"Fathers teach us the true meaning of resilience."

What kinds of games did you play together?

....

....

....

....

What qualities did you look for in a friend? Has that changed?

....

....

....

....

....

....

Did you have any sleepovers or holidays together?

....

....

Childhood

"A father's guidance is a gift that lasts a lifetime."

School Days

What do you remember about your first day of school? What have you been told about how you felt?

....

....

....

....

....

....

....

....

Was your school nearby; did you walk or cycle or was it further away?

....

....

Childhood

"Dads may not wear capes, but they are heroes every day."

Do you have any memories of your first teacher/s? Was there something special about one of them that stood out?

....

....

....

....

....

Did you enjoy sports or were you more of an introverted child who preferred books and drawing?

....

....

Many people remember their school dinners or packed lunches; do you remember anything about them?

....

....

....

....

Childhood

"A father's heart is a child's safe place to land."

Did you wear a uniform to school or was it more casual? What colour was your school uniform if you wore one?

....

....

What are some of your favourite memories about your early days at school?

....

....

....

....

....

....

....

Did you join any groups, like Rainbows, Brownies or Girl Guides?

....

....

Becoming Yourself

"Dads are the silent architects of our dreams."

How would you describe yourself when you were a young child? Were you shy, confident, sporty or a good friend?

....

....

....

....

....

....

What sort of things did you used to worry about that turned out to be less serious than you thought at the time?

....

....

....

....

....

....

Becoming Yourself

"A father's wisdom is the map to his children's future."

Did you have a favourite book or comic?

....

Was there a song that you remember playing on the radio a lot? Did you know all the words to a particular song?

....

What did you want to be when you grew up?

....

....

....

....

....

....

Did you make a specific wish when you blew out your birthday candles? Maybe you wanted to be invisible or have the ability to fly?

....

....

....

Becoming Yourself

"Behind every great person stands a loving father."

What superhero did you want to be and why?

....

....

....

....

What was something that scared you as a child? Are you still scared of it?

....

....

....

....

Can you remember your most embarrassing moment, for example, did you call your teacher Mum?

....

....

....

....

Becoming Yourself

"A dad's love knows no boundaries, only endless devotion."

Was there something that you wished you could do? Was there something you really wanted to be better at?

....

....

....

....

....

....

....

....

What made you laugh?

....

....

....

....

Becoming Yourself

"A father's hug is the world's most comforting place."

Who were your first role models, and why?

....

....

....

....

Did you have a pet? Did you have a favourite animal, and are they still your favourite animal or has that changed?

....

....

....

What do you think was your natural talent? What did you begin to discover you were very good at?

....

....

....

....

Becoming Yourself

"Dads are the silent warriors of every family."

What kind of sweets or candy did you eat when you were young?

....

....

....

....

What did you do at the weekends?

....

....

....

....

....

....

....

....

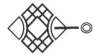 # Teen Life

"A father's laughter is the music that makes memories last."

Family Life

When you became a teenager, did you find yourself getting along better with a particular family member? Why?

....

....

....

....

....

....

....

Did you get into trouble as a teenager? Would you describe yourself as rebellious or obedient?

....

....

....

....

 # Teen Life

"A dad's love is like a steady wind, pushing us forward."

Were your parent/s strict? What types of punishment did your parents use when you were a teenager?

....
....
....
....
....
....
....

Who, do you think, had the biggest influence on you? Did you have a hero or someone to look up to?

....
....
....
....

 # Teen Life

"The best things a dad can give are his time and love."

Do you think teenagers today have it too easy in comparison to your teenage life?

....

....

....

Did you do any chores around the house?

....

....

Did you get 'pocket-money' or take on a part-time job?

....

....

Did you live in a city? Do you think it is better to raise teenagers in the city, a small town, or the country?

....

....

....

 # Teen Life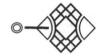

"Dads lead by example, showing us the power of kindness."

What sort of traditions did you have? What did you do at family events or religious holidays?

....

....

....

....

....

....

....

....

....

....

....

....

....

....

Teen Life

"Fathers are the unsung heroes behind every success story."

Relationships

People say that your friends are the most important people in your life as a teenager. Do you agree?

....

....

Did you have many friends or just one or two?

....

What qualities did you look for in a friend? Was it popularity or something else?

....

....

....

How would you describe yourself as a friend when you were a teenager?

....

....

....

 # Teen Life

"A father's love is the anchor that keeps us grounded."

Did you go out a lot? Did you have a curfew?

....

....

What places did you go to? Did you go dancing or to music events?

....

....

....

....

Were your teenage friendships fun or would you describe them as quite stressful?

....

....

....

....

....

Teen Life

"In a father's arms, we learn the meaning of strength."

Did you have a girl/boyfriend when you were a teenager? What were they like?

....
....
....
....
....

How did you and your fellow teens go about forming relationships?

....
....
....
....
....
....
....

Teen Life

"A dad's patience is a lesson in true love."

Lessons Learned

What was it like to be a teenager in your society?

....

....

....

....

....

What piece of advice were you given that has stayed with you?

....

....

....

....

....

Father, Share Your Story

 # Teen Life

"A father's support is the foundation of every dream."

Did you have an embarrassing moment that you still tell people about today?

....

....

....

....

....

....

Would you rather be a child, teenager or an adult? Why?

....

....

....

....

....

....

Teen Life

"Dads are proof that love is both gentle and strong."

Did you know what you wanted to do when you left school or did going into the wide world worry you?

....

....

....

....

As a teenager, how did you dress? Was fashion important to you?

....

....

Do you think the teenage trends were better then?

....

....

What kinds of clothes did you wear that you now laugh about?

....

....

Teen Life

"A father's words are seeds of wisdom that grow with us."

Were you affected by the media? Was there something in the news that you remember having an impact on you?

....

....

....

....

If you could do something differently, what would you change about your teen years?

....

....

....

....

....

....

....

 # Teen Life

"A dad's strength lies in his love, not his power."

Do you think that school taught you valuable lessons or did you learn more outside of the classroom?

....

....

Who was the best teacher you had at the time and why?

....

....

....

....

....

....

Did you get into trouble at school? Did you find school interesting?

....

....

....

Teen Life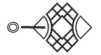

"A father's love shapes us into who we're meant to be."

What was the most difficult rule you had to abide by? Did you disagree with it?

....
....
....

What were you most looking forward to about becoming an adult?

....
....
....
....

Was there something you were not looking forward to about adulthood?

....
....
....
....

Beginning Adult Life

"Fathers plant the seeds of love and watch us bloom."

Passions and Pursuits

Did you know what career, if any, you would like when you left school?

....

....

Did you pursue something you were good at, something you loved or something you believed would be a sensible career path?

....

....

What subjects did you take when you began to specialise? Did you go to college or university?

....

....

Did you study for many years, or did you go almost immediately into a job? Why?

....

....

....

Beginning Adult Life

"Dads are the silent champions of family and love."

Did you learn to drive? If you did, what do you remember about it?

....

....

....

....

Did you continue the same hobbies as when you were younger or did your interests change when you left school?

....

....

Did you have a goal for your life? Was there something that you were passionate about achieving?

....

....

....

....

....

....

Beginning Adult Life

"A father's belief in us helps us believe in ourselves."

How would you describe your first year after you left school?

....
....
....
....
....
....
....
....

What was your first job like? Did you enjoy it?

....
....
....
....

Beginning Adult Life

"Every hug from a father feels like a promise of forever."

What kind of environment did you want to work in? For example, did you want to work in an office or outside?

....

....

....

....

What challenges did you need to overcome when you left school?

....

....

....

What did you hope your future would look like? Did you have a particular lifestyle in mind or a particular place you wanted to live in?

....

....

....

....

Beginning Adult Life

"A dad's legacy is one of kindness, strength, and courage."

Who do you believe was your biggest influence and support? What support did they give you?

....

....

....

....

....

....

What responsibilities were you juggling? How did you overcome this?

....

....

....

....

....

....

Beginning Adult Life

"A father's love is a light that never fades."

Values, Hopes and Dreams

What made you happy? What were you most excited about as you embarked on adult life?

....

....

....

....

What activities or experiences do you remember being especially valuable?

....

....

....

....

Did you have a plan for your life or did you 'wing it'?

....

....

Beginning Adult Life

"Dads give us the courage to face life with a smile."

What were your special talents?

....

....

What did people most like about you? Were you a helpful or supportive friend? Or were you fun to be with?

....

....

....

What were your biggest fears?

....

....

....

....

....

....

Beginning Adult Life

"A father's advice is the gift that keeps on giving."

Can you remember a special achievement? What achievement were you most proud of and why?

....

....

....

What was the worst piece of advice you were given about career or starting adult life?

....

....

....

....

What did you dream of becoming? Did you ever want to be famous?

....

....

....

....

Beginning Adult Life

"Fathers make us feel loved, protected, and unstoppable."

Was there something you really wanted to do to change the world? What kinds of things did you think needed to change?

....

....

....

....

Many people look back at who they were when they left school and cringe! What do you look back on and laugh about?

....

....

....

....

What kind of person were you and have you changed much?

....

....

....

....

Adult Relationships

"A father's hands may be rough, but his heart is pure gold."

Family Relationships

Would you describe yourself as someone who was eager to leave your family and start life independently?

....

....

Was leaving home emotional? Did you move far away?

....

....

Did you maintain a close relationship with your parents and siblings when you left home?

....

....

Did your family help you get your life off the ground, or did you do it all yourself? How do you feel about that?

....

....

....

Adult Relationships

"Dads teach us that strength and love go hand in hand."

Was there someone in your family you found inspiring? Someone you wanted to follow in the footsteps of? If so, why?

....

....

....

....

Did you find yourself diverging from your family's values? In what way?

....

....

....

....

What memories do you have of your first home away from home? Did anyone help you fix it up?

....

....

....

....

Adult Relationships

"A father's love is steady, unwavering, and true."

Romance & Relationships

Did you have a steady girlfriend/boyfriend? If so, how did you meet and did you stay together long?

....

....

....

Did you find it easy to meet people? Why or why not?

....

....

....

What kind of social life did you have? Where did you meet people? Did you have lots of places to go?

....

....

....

....

....

Adult Relationships

"With a dad's love, we can face anything life brings."

What do you remember most about your first romantic relationships?

....

....

....

....

Did you go on any holidays with your girl/boyfriend? Where did you go and what was it like?

....

....

....

What did you learn about romance and love from your first relationships?

....

....

....

....

....

Adult Relationships

"Dads don't just tell us how to live; they show us."

Did your family like your friends or partners? Did they meet them?

....

....

Did your friends cause any conflicts about your romantic relationships? What happened?

....

....

....

....

What kinds of things did you spend your time doing with your partner or friends?

....

....

....

....

....

....

Adult Relationships

"A father's love is a gift we cherish forever."

Would you describe yourself as very social or too busy with your career or job for socialising?

....

....

Can you remember a special gift you were given by a romantic partner or friend?

....

....

Do you remember when you first fell in love?

....

....

Where were you when you had your first kiss?

....

....

Are you still friends with the same people now?

....

....

Adult Relationships

"Dads are the foundation upon which we build our dreams."

Can you remember any funny stories about your first relationships?

....
....
....
....

What was the craziest thing you did together?

....
....
....
....

Did you have any adventures? Perhaps you went somewhere and found yourself facing the unexpected!

....
....

Were you the quiet one in the group, or were you the life and soul of the party?

....

 # Adulthood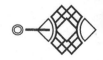

"Fathers are the quiet heroes who never stop giving."

Challenges and Obstacles

What did you most appreciate about life as an adult compared to life as a child?

....
....
....
....
....
....

What were some of the main challenges you faced as a young adult?

....
....
....
....
....
....

Adulthood

"A dad's love is a guiding star in every child's life."

How did the pressure to find a stable career or manage the home affect your outlook on life?

....

....

....

....

Did you manage to maintain a healthy work-life balance? How did you do it, if so?

....

....

....

....

Do you remember a particularly nerve-racking event that you thought would be worse than it was? Maybe you had to give a speech or presentation?

....

....

....

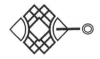 # Adulthood

"In a father's smile, we find joy and safety."

What was the best interview you ever went to? Why was it so good?

....

....

....

....

Was there a job interview that went terribly wrong? What happened?

....

....

....

....

What major decisions did you have to make and how did you go about making them?

....

....

....

....

 # Adulthood

"Dads are the strength behind every child's laughter."

Did you face any obstacles in establishing new relationships or maintaining old ones during this stage of life?

....

....

Did you overcome any challenges in your romantic relationships? What did you learn from them?

....

....

....

....

What were some of the obstacles you faced in terms of pursuing your personal goals or passions?

....

....

....

....

....

Adulthood

"A father's love whispers, 'You're safe here.'"

How did you manage to forge your own identity in adulthood?

....

....

....

....

Did you deviate from the norm? Or were you keen to fit in with your peers?

....

....

Beliefs and Values

It can be hard to stick to your beliefs as a young adult. Can you remember a time when that was tested, either at work or in your relationships?

....

....

....

....

Adulthood

"Dads are the protectors of both hearts and dreams."

What do you remember noticing about the way your friendships changed? Did you still meet up with your friends?

....

....

....

....

Can you remember a place you used to go to that always made you smile?

....

....

....

....

How did you relax? What sorts of things did you do to unwind?

....

....

....

....

 # Adulthood

"A father's presence is the foundation of confidence."

What was most important to you? Can you think of any examples of how your values affected your choices?

....

....

....

....

Were you politically engaged? Did you have any special causes with which you were involved?

....

....

....

....

What energised you? What excited you? What made you feel most satisfied?

....

....

....

....

 # Adulthood

"Fathers are proof that love and strength can be one."

Where did your values come from? What stories about other peoples' lives influenced your values?

....

....

....

....

Did you begin to establish some of your own traditions at this age? What were they?

....

....

....

....

Did you feel any pressure to compete with other people or were you your own person?

....

....

....

....

Adulthood

"A dad's love gives us wings to fly and roots to stay."

Lifestyle

What was going on around the world that concerned you or bothered you?

....

....

....

....

Was there a celebrity you admired? Why did you admire them?

....

....

Did you have a favourite actor or actress? What films were they in that you loved?

....

....

Did you spend a lot of time listening to music? How did you listen to music? Did you have a Walkman, CD player or some other device?

....

....

 # Adulthood

"A father's love is a melody of kindness and strength."

Where was your favourite place to go on holiday? Why?

....

....

....

....

Did you live in a house or a flat?

....

....

Did you share a house? What were some of the funny things that happened with your housemates, if so?

....

....

....

....

....

....

Adulthood

"Dads give us strength when we need it most."

Can you remember what you loved most about being independent or having your own home?

....

....

....

....

....

....

Did you enjoy nature or were you more of a city person?

....

....

Were there any noticeable changes in your society in comparison to when you were a child?

....

....

....

....

 # The People Who Shape Us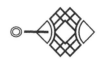

"In a father's embrace, we feel unbreakable."

Was there someone in your life who influenced you greatly at the time? Perhaps it was a boss or a colleague?

....

....

Did you get along with your work colleagues? Do you remember any particularly funny moments with them?

....

....

....

....

Were you friends with the people you worked with or was your friendship group separate to your work?

....

....

How influenced were you by your family? In what ways?

....

....

 # The People Who Shape Us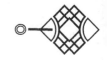

"A father's wisdom shapes us even after he's gone."

Did something your family said in the past become more meaningful to you as an adult?

....

....

....

....

Can you remember a conversation or some words of wisdom that changed the way you saw yourself?

....

....

....

....

Did you ever read a book or see a film that influenced you to change the way you lived your life?

....

....

....

The People Who Shape Us

"Dads teach us to stand tall and dream big."

Who was a bad influence on you? Why?

....
....
....
....
....

Who taught you a very important lesson about finances? What was it and how did you learn it?

....
....
....
....
....
....
....

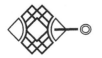 # The People Who Shape Us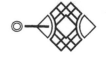

"A father's love stays with us, always and forever."

Did anyone make you change your mind about something you had always believed? Who and what was it?

....

....

....

....

Who do you think taught you about the meaning of success? What did they teach you?

....

....

....

....

Do you remember if there was anyone who you wished you were more like? What was it about them that you wanted to learn?

....

....

....

Father, Share Your Story

 # The People Who Shape Us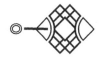

"Fathers give us the courage to conquer our fears."

Did you surround yourself with people who had a lot in common with you or with people who were very different?

....

....

Who made you believe in yourself? Did anyone help to build your self-esteem? How?

....

....

....

....

What made you doubt yourself? Did anyone shake your confidence in who you were? How did you overcome it?

....

....

....

....

 # The People Who Shape Us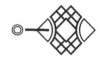

"A dad's love is like a lighthouse, guiding us home."

Did you find younger people or older people more inspiring? Why?

....

....

....

....

Who was the first person to give you that all important break in life? What did they do?

....

....

....

....

Did anyone try to stop you achieving your goals? What did you do about it?

....

....

....

Father, Share Your Story

 # The People Who Shape Us

"Dads are the hidden heroes behind every success."

Can you remember any special moments that defined you?

....

....

....

....

Was there someone in your life who always encouraged you to push yourself outside of your comfort zone?

....

....

Can you remember any silly mistakes you made that you managed to turn into a great lesson?

....

....

....

....

....

 # Fatherhood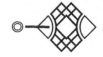

"A father's wisdom becomes our greatest strength."

First Moments

Where were you when you found out that you were going to be a father?

....

....

Can you remember how you felt? What were you excited about? What terrified you?

....

....

....

....

How did you prepare for parenthood? Were there any books that you read or tasks you had to complete to help prepare?

....

....

....

....

Fatherhood

"Dads teach us that kindness is the greatest strength."

What advice did people give you about becoming a father? Were they right?

....

....

....

....

....

....

Were you there for the birth of your first child? How did you feel and what did you do?

....

....

....

....

....

....

....

Fatherhood

"A father's love builds unbreakable bonds."

What do you remember most about your first day as a father?

....

....

....

....

....

....

....

....

How did you decide on the name of your child? Did you name them after someone or did the name have a special meaning?

....

....

....

....

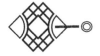 # Fatherhood

"Dads are the glue that holds a family together."

What kinds of conversations did you have about raising your child? Who were they with?

....

....

....

....

....

....

Do you remember the first gift you gave your child? Was it when they were born?

....

....

Who helped you settle into parenthood that first month?

....

....

....

....

Fatherhood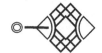

"A father's strength lies in his heart, not his fists."

Did you have any time away from work or did you have to go back to work immediately?

....

....

How did you cope with the lack of sleep? Did you help with night-time feeding or changing?

....

....

....

....

....

Did your family and friends celebrate with you? How?

....

....

....

....

....

Fatherhood

"Dads believe in us even when we don't believe in ourselves."

Traditions

What family traditions did you establish that were your very own?

....

....

....

....

....

....

Did you continue any family traditions that you valued as a child yourself? What were they?

....

....

....

....

....

....

 # Fatherhood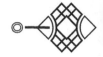

"A father's love is the foundation of every great story."

Can you remember what goals you had when you became a father?

....

....

....

....

How would you describe your first year of parenthood? What were you like?

....

....

....

....

Can you remember anything specific that you were shocked by or that you were not expecting?

....

....

....

....

Fatherhood

"Dads show us that real strength is found in love."

What was the most rewarding part of your first year as a parent?

....

....

....

....

How did your friends react to you becoming a father? Did they support you?

....

....

....

....

Did you make any big changes to your life? What were they and why did you make them?

....

....

....

....

Reflections

"A father's hug says, 'I'm here for you.'"

If there was one thing you could go back and do again, what would it be?

....

....

What advice would you give your teenage self? Why?

....

....

....

....

....

Is there anything you would change about your first years at work?

....

....

....

....

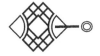 # Reflections

"Dads are our first teachers, guiding us with love."

How have you grown as a parent? In what ways are you different now compared to when you first became a father?

....

....

....

....

Whose advice was the most helpful when you became a father?

....

....

What have you learned about being a father since the early days?

....

....

....

....

....

 # Reflections

"A father's love is quiet, steady, and strong."

Is there anything you want to do that you have not done yet? How could you go about making it happen?

....

....

....

....

....

....

What do you miss most about your younger years?

....

....

....

....

....

Reflections

"Fathers shape our lives with love and care."

What would you say to your younger self about growing up?

....

....

....

....

....

....

....

Have things gone the way you expected in your life, or has it been a whirlwind of unpredictability?

....

....

....

....

....

Notes to Loved Ones

"Dads are the silent warriors of our hearts."

To whom would you love to express your gratitude to, if you could? Perhaps a teacher or an old boss?

....

....

....

....

Is there someone from your past you would dearly love to apologise to?

....

....

What would you say to your first love if you met them now?

....

....

....

....

....

Notes to Loved Ones

"A father's patience is the greatest act of love."

Do you have any friends that you lost contact with and would love to strike up a friendship with? What would you like to talk to them about?

....

....

....

....

....

....

If you could go back and tell your child one thing that you didn't say when they were younger what would it be?

....

....

....

....

....

....

Notes to Loved Ones

"Dads teach us the power of resilience and grace."

If you could send a message or a letter to your parent/s what would you write?

....

....

....

....

....

....

....

....

....

....

....

....

....

Notes to Loved Ones

"A father's love is a guiding force in every child's life."

Perhaps something remains unsaid between you and your sibling/s. Were you to say one thing or set something straight, what would you admit?

....

....

....

....

....

....

Did you keep a secret from someone? Who was it and would you like to tell it now?

....

....

....

....

....

....

 # Fun Insights

"In a father's eyes, we find love and hope."

What's a hidden talent or skill you have that most people don't know about?

....

....

If you could live in any other decade, which one would you choose and why?

....

....

....

....

What's the most adventurous thing you've ever done?

....

....

....

....

....

Fun Insights

"Dads teach us that true strength lies in kindness."

If you could learn a new language, which one would it be and why?

....
....

What's the best surprise you've ever received?

....
....
....
....

Have you ever met someone famous? If so, what was the experience like?

....
....
....
....
....

 # Fun Insights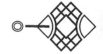

"A father's love knows no boundaries."

What's a book, movie, or TV show that you think everyone should experience?

....

....

If you could master any musical instrument, which would it be and why?

....

....

....

What's the most unusual job you've ever had?

....

....

....

What's a piece of technology or gadget you wish had existed when you were younger?

....

....

 # Fun Insights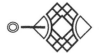

"Dads give us roots to grow and wings to soar."

What's the most memorable meal you've ever had?

....

....

If you could design your perfect day, what would it look like?

....

....

....

....

....

....

....

....

....

....

 # Fun Insights

"A father's advice becomes our strength."

What's something you've always wanted to try but haven't gotten the chance to yet?

....

....

....

....

....

If you could trade lives with someone for a day, who would it be and why?

....

....

....

....

....

....

 # Fun Insights

"Dads show us how to love deeply and live boldly."

What's the funniest or strangest thing that's ever happened to you?

....

....

....

....

....

....

Is there a historical event you wish you could have witnessed in person?

....

....

....

....

....

....

Fun Insights

"A father's hug is worth a thousand words."

What's a family tradition from your childhood that you've always cherished?

....

....

....

....

....

....

If you could visit any country in the world, where would you go and what would you do?

....

....

....

....

....

....

....

Fun Insights

"Dads give us the courage to follow our dreams."

What's the kindest thing a stranger has ever done for you?

....

....

....

....

....

....

What's a motto or piece of advice that you've found to be most meaningful in your life?

....

....

....

....

....

....

 # Notes to Family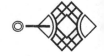

"A father's love is the foundation of every family."

Father, Share Your Story

 # Notes to Family

"Dads are the quiet protectors of our happiness."

 # Notes to Family

"A father's heart is the foundation of our lives."

Father, Share Your Story

 # Notes to Family

"Dads teach us that love is stronger than fear."

Notes to Family

"A father's love is a compass for every life journey."

Notes to Family

"Dads inspire us to live with courage and kindness."

Father, Share Your Story

 # Notes to Family

"A father's strength lies in his love and wisdom."

Notes to Family

"Dads are the silent heroes we look up to."

 # Notes to Family

"A father's love is the gift that keeps us going."

Notes to Family

"Dads guide us with love, patience, and grace."

Notes to Family

"A father's love is the heartbeat of a family."

Notes to Family

"Dads teach us to be strong, yet gentle."

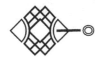 # Notes to Friends

"A father's love is the true foundation of courage."

Notes to Friends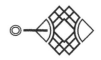

"Dads are our biggest supporters and greatest protectors."

 # Notes to Friends

"A father's wisdom becomes our inner strength."

Notes to Friends

"Dads teach us the art of living with integrity."

 # Notes to Friends

"A father's love is a constant, never-changing force."

Notes to Friends

"Dads show us that true heroes wear love on their sleeves."

 # Notes to Friends

"A father's love is a gentle, guiding hand."

Father, Share Your Story

 # Notes to Friends

"Dads are the anchors in life's stormiest seas."

Father, Share Your Story

 # Notes to Friends

"A father's wisdom is a priceless gift."

Notes to Friends

"Dads give us the courage to reach for the stars."

Notes to Friends

"A father's love is the greatest gift life can give."

Made in the USA
Las Vegas, NV
14 April 2025